83-1752

j599
LAU   Lauber, Patricia

Great whales

DATE		
DEC 27 '83	SEP 6 1988	JUN 22 1995
FEB 21 1984	APR 15 1988	FEB 03 1996
MAR 10 1984	JUN 10 1988	AUG 11 1996
JUL 20 198	JUN 11 1988	
OCT 20 198	MAR 10 1990	MAY 11 1998
NOV 7 198	APR 26 1991	NOV 06 2000
JAN 2 1985	MAY 19 199	
JAN 19 1985		JUN 24 2010
JAN 19 1985	MAY 17 1994	
	AUG 25 1994	
FEB 19 1985	JAN 27 1995	

GREAT WHALES

Relatively little is known about great whales or their ecological role, for they are the hardest of all mammals to study. It is difficult to track and observe them in their natural environment, and adult whales are too big to keep and study in captivity. The whole story of the great whales may never be known, for overhunting has brought many species to the edge of extinction.

In this succinct, interesting book, the author gives a simple and appreciative account of the great whales: what we do and don't know about them and their chances for continuing survival. She describes recent discoveries—the songs of the humpback whales and echolocation in the sperm whales—and ends with the true and charming story of a young gray whale that made friends with two human beings.

GREAT
WHALES

By Patricia Lauber

GARRARD PUBLISHING COMPANY
CHAMPAIGN, ILLINOIS

Photo Credits

Jen and Des Bartlett from Bruce Coleman: p. 38
John Dominis from Time-LIFE Picture Agency, 1972,
   © Time, Inc.: pp. 40–41
Robert Hermes from National Audubon Society: p. 21
Stephen Leatherwood, San Diego: pp. 2, 6, 19, 32
Stephen Leatherwoood, courtesy of Naval Undersea Center,
   San Diego: p. 63
Marineland of Florida, St. Augustine: pp. 9, 11
Miami Seaquarium: p. 29
Avis Reeves from National Audubon Society: p. 20
John Seeker, courtesy of Sea World, San Diego: pp. 17, 52,
   55, 57, 58, 59, 60 (both)
Gordon Williamson from Bruce Coleman: pp. 47, 49

Illustrations

The drawings on pages 14, 27, 34–35, and 43 are from the book
The Great Whales, copyright © 1973, 1974 by Faith McNulty.
Reprinted by permission of Doubleday and Co., Inc.

The drawings on page 16 are by Edward Malsberg.

The cover painting is by Victor Mays.

Library of Congress Cataloging in Publication Data

Lauber, Patricia.
   Great whales.

   (Good earth)
   SUMMARY: Describes the characteristics and behavior
of different kinds of whales and discusses why they
are threatened by extinction.
   1. Whales—Juvenile literature. [1. Whales.]
I. Title.
QL737.C4L28   599'.51   74–28231
ISBN 0–8116–6103–2

Cover:
A humpback whale and her calf. Note their lumps and
white fins. No other whales are marked this way.

Title Page:
Spy-hopping: Gray whale pops up out of the water
and seems to take a look around.

CONTENTS

1. THE GRAY WHALES

"The whales are here!"

Every winter this news draws crowds to cliffs along the California coast. From them, people can watch the whales go by. It is a sight to remember. Powerful tails pump. Long, dark bodies slide through the water. Whales dive, surface, and spout. For days on end the whales go by.

The passing whales are California gray whales. They are some of the world's great whales, which means they are big whales. Adult gray whales are

Gray whales are counted from the air as they pass along the California coast.

40 to 45 feet long. That is longer than two big station wagons.

The whales are coming from their feeding grounds in the far north. With the start of autumn, they head south on a voyage that is thousands of miles long. The leading whales are females that will soon give birth. For them, there is no time to waste. A calf, or baby whale, might die if it is born in cold, rough waters.

By December, the first whales are passing San Diego. They are nearing the warm, shallow bays of Baja California. One of these bays is called Scammon Lagoon. It is the main breeding ground of the California gray whales. Here the calves are born soon after the whales arrive.

No one has ever seen the birth of

A baby dolphin is born tail first, as shown here. Probably all baby whales are born this way.

a gray whale or any other great whale. But scientists have watched the birth of dolphins, which are small whales. They think that all baby whales are born in the same way— tail first.

Marineland of Florida

There is a good reason for this. Whales are not fish, as some people think. They belong to the class of animals called mammals. Horses, dogs, cows, cats, and mice are mammals. So are elephants and rabbits. And so are we.

All mammals breathe air. If they breathe water, they drown.

A baby whale is born in water. It must not start to breathe there. It must not breathe before it reaches the surface. And so it is born tail first— or head last. As soon as the head is free, the mother pushes her baby to the surface. There the baby whale takes its first breath.

A newborn gray whale looks very much like its mother, except that it is smaller. Even so, it is a big baby. It

Baby dolphin feeds underwater on its mother's milk.
All baby whales feed in this same way.

is twelve to seventeen feet long. It weighs between 1,500 and 3,000 pounds.

Mammals nurse their young on milk. The gray whale nurses her baby in the water. She squirts milk into its mouth. The young whale feeds, then surfaces to breathe.

A whale's milk is very rich and the

baby grows quickly. It gains 200 to 400 pounds a week.

A gray whale nurses her calf for a number of months. During this time, the young whale never strays far from its mother. Usually it swims close beside her. The mother takes great care of her calf. She will not leave it if it is in trouble. Another female may help her take care of the calf. This female is known as an aunt. The aunt is a whale that does not have a calf of her own.

Each winter about half the females have calves. The other females are being courted and are mating.

In courtship the big whales churn the water. They rise and fall. They wave their long flippers in the air. When the courting ends, mating takes place. These females will bear their calves the following winter. A gray whale usually has one calf every two years.

The gray whales spend about two months in the lagoon. They give birth and mate. They also play in the water, swimming and rolling over. They ride the surf at the lagoon's opening. They spy-hop—popping up and seeming to look around. Big males leap all the way out of the water and fall back with a crash.

This is also a time for sleeping. Whales sleep in short naps, the way cattle do. A sleeping whale floats like a log, drifting with the tide.

The whales need their rest. The coming of spring means that it is time to start a long voyage north.

2. THE LONG TRIP NORTH

All great whales are long-distance swimmers. But gray whales swim the farthest. Each year they make a round trip of about 10,000 miles. They swim from where they breed to where they feed and back again.

Like all whales, a gray whale swims by pumping its tail up and down. It uses its flippers to keep its balance and to help steer. A gray whale's

A gray whale (above) may grow to be 40 to 45 feet long.

body has the shape of a torpedo. The skin is thin and as smooth as glass. The smooth, streamlined body slides through the water.

The gray whale is not one of the fastest swimmers. It cruises at a speed of about five miles an hour. But on a long trip, it swims quite steadily. Gray whales swim both day and night. No one knows how much they rest or if they stop to eat.

Three months of swimming brings the gray whales to a place that is rich in food. They are in their summer feeding grounds in the waters of the Arctic.

Here there are huge masses of tiny floating plants. These plants thrive in the cold Arctic water. Also, Arctic summer days are very long. There is plenty of sunlight. The tiny plants multiply rapidly.

These plants form a large supply of food for tiny sea creatures such as water fleas, sea butterflies, and shrimplike animals. These tiny creatures are known as krill.

With a good supply of food, krill multiply rapidly. Huge clouds of them

Whale food: shrimplike creature of the Antarctic (top), sea butterfly and water flea of the Arctic (bottom left and right). All are shown much larger than they are.

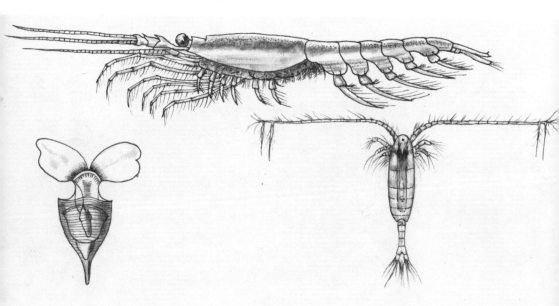

The mustache-strainer of this young gray whale traps food in its mouth, while water is squirted out.

float in the water. And they are food for the gray whales. The whales feed by straining krill out of water.

Gray whales have no teeth. Instead, each has what looks like a huge, hairy mustache. It grows from the gum of the whale's upper jaw. The mustache acts as a strainer. A whale swims through a patch of krill with its mouth open. The mouth fills with krill and seawater. The whale closes its mouth and raises its tongue. The water squirts out through the strainer, but the krill is trapped in the mouth. The whale swallows its food and takes another mouthful.

The mustache-strainer looks hairy, but it is not made of hair. It is sometimes called whalebone, but it is not made of bone either. It is made of a horny material, like that in our fingernails or in the hoofs of cattle. The best name for it is baleen.

A whale has 200 to 300 blades of baleen. The inside edges of the blades are fringed with bristles. The bristles give baleen its hairy look. They are excellent for trapping krill.

The great clouds of krill are fairly near the sea's surface. They are

Gray whale dives, showing broad, strong tail.

between 30 and 300 feet down. A gray whale reaches its food by diving. Before diving, it fills its lungs with air.

Whales breathe through blowholes. A gray whale has two blowholes. They are slits set in the top of the head. A blowhole has elastic sides that snap shut to keep out water.

At the surface, a gray whale takes several slow, deep breaths. Its back curves and the whale disappears in a dive. It feeds underwater for four to seven minutes. Then it surfaces, breathes slowly, and dives again.

When a whale surfaces, air rushes out of its lungs. The whale's breath is

Gray whales spouting as they reach the surface.

Squid come in many sizes and exist in huge numbers.

warm and moist. As it strikes the air above the ocean, it is cooled. The moisture in it turns to little drops of water. The breath can then be seen. It looks like a spout of water. The spout may also hold a little oily foam.

The gray whales spend four months feeding in the Arctic. Krill is their main food, but they may also swallow fish and squid. Squid are sea creatures that are related to the octopus.

After a summer of feeding, the gray whales have grown plump. Their bodies are covered by a thick, firm layer of fat. This fat is called blubber. It serves a whale in several ways.

Blubber fills out a whale's body and gives it a shape that slides through the water.

Blubber is light enough to float in water. It helps keep a whale afloat.

Blubber is the chief thing that keeps a whale warm. Because they are mammals, whales are warm-blooded. That is, their bodies make heat. Every mammal needs a way of holding its body heat. For a whale, blubber does this job. It seals in the heat made by the whale's body.

Blubber is also a supply of food. A whale can live off its fat at times when it is not feeding. Blubber is the chief fuel for a gray whale's body on the long trip south.

Blubber is very important to the life of a gray whale. Yet blubber has cost many a gray whale its life. The reason is that blubber is rich in oil. A big whale has far more oil-rich blubber than a small whale. Its blubber made the gray whale a prize for whale hunters.

Twice hunters almost wiped out the California gray whales. Twice the whales were able to come back, perhaps because they were whales that stayed together. They could find mates even when their numbers were small. In their second comeback, they were helped by laws.

Now no one may hunt the gray

whales in their breeding grounds. There is no hunting off the California coast.

There is not supposed to be any hunting in the Arctic. Even so, Russian ships are hunting gray whales there. The Russians say they are taking only a few whales. But no one knows if this is true.

A different kind of danger may lie in Baja California. This desert land is being opened up. Roads, motels, and houses are being built. No one knows if this will harm or change the breeding grounds.

Still, for now, the California gray whales are safe. Once there were only a few hundred of them left. Today they number between 8,000 and 12,000. They may be the safest of all the really big whales.

3. THE GREAT WHALES

There are many kinds of whales in the seas. In all, there are about 100 kinds. To sort them out, scientists begin by dividing them into two main groups.

One group is made up of whales with teeth. These are called toothed whales. Toothed whales feed mostly on fish and squid. A toothed whale has one blowhole. The males of this group are bigger than the females.

The second group is made up of whales that have baleen in place of teeth. These are called baleen whales. They feed chiefly on krill. A baleen whale has two blowholes. Females are bigger than males.

Most of the world's whales are toothed whales. And nearly all of these are small whales. The best known toothed whales are the dolphins, porpoises, killer whales, and pilot whales.

Among the toothed whales there is only one giant, only one great whale. This is the sperm whale. Males grow 55 to 60 feet long.

A sperm whale has a huge head that is somewhat square in shape. The big forehead is filled with a fine, pure, waxy oil. It holds hundreds of gallons of this oil. The whale's blubber holds still more oil.

The lower jaw is long and narrow.

All the teeth are in this jaw. There are about 40 of them. Each tooth is as big as a man's fist.

A sperm whale probably uses its teeth in catching squid, which are its main food. But it does not use its teeth for chewing. It swallows its food whole.

Males also use their teeth in fighting. They fight to win females.

Sperm whales live in herds. Each

Male sperm whales grow to a length of about 60 feet.

herd has a group of females and their calves. It is led by one big male. The male mates with all the females in his herd.

Young males live in the herd until they leave their mothers. Then they also leave the herd. They stay with other young males until they win herds of their own.

Sperm whales are found in all the oceans of the world. The herds usually stay in fairly warm waters, moving about in search of food. But in summer some sperm whales hunt food in cold waters near the poles. These whales are males without herds.

Sperm whales are not very fast swimmers. But of all whales they are the champion divers. They can dive to depths of 3,000 feet and more. They

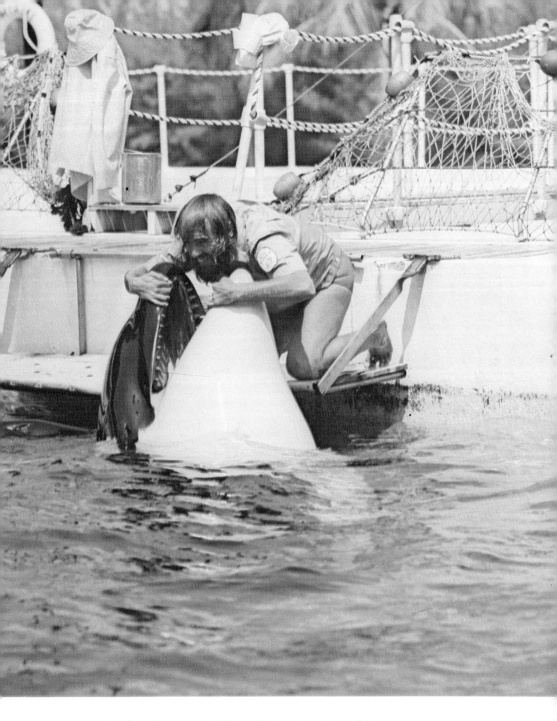

Another discovery: Killer whales, long feared by men,
have proved to be friendly and gentle in captivity.
This is one of the small toothed whales.

dive in search of giant squid and other creatures on the ocean bottom.

When they are not hunting food, sperm whales usually stay near the surface. They can swim at the surface or underwater. Swimming or diving, a big male can stay underwater for about an hour.

How does a sperm whale find its way underwater? How does a herd stay together? How does a calf find its mother? How do the whales find their food?

For a long time, these were puzzling questions. The underwater world is largely dark. Near the surface there is some light. A whale can probably see what is about 60 to 100 feet away. But the deeper a whale goes, the less light there is. How do sperm whales find squid in the pitch-black of 3,000 feet?

They do it with sounds.

People have long known that sperm whales make noises. To our ears these noises sound like bangs, thuds, creaks, or knocks. But scientists have taped these sounds, then played the tapes very slowly. The tapes show that each noise is made up of a number of very quick clicks.

A sperm whale sends out these bursts of clicks. The clicks travel through the water. When they hit something, they bounce back. The whale hears the echoes. Different kinds of echoes come back. The echo from a squid is different than the echo from a rock on the ocean floor.

That is how a sperm whale finds

In warm waters pests such as barnacles and sea lice (shown above) attach themselves to whales. In cold waters they drop off, leaving patchy scars on the skin.

its food. That is how it finds its way. That is how sperm whales find each other. Scientists think that each whale has its own pattern of clicks. If so, that is how a calf can find its own mother in the herd. It knows the sounds she makes.

For some years scientists have known that dolphins use clicks and echoes. The discovery that sperm whales also do this is new. So far no one fully understands how the whales send out their clicks. But it seems likely that the oil in their heads plays a part in this. If so, another puzzle will be solved. It is: Why do sperm whales have oil in their heads?

Do all whales send out clicks? That is something else no one knows. All whales must have some way of finding food. They must have some way of keeping in touch. But among the baleen whales, only one is known to make much noise.

4. MORE GREAT WHALES

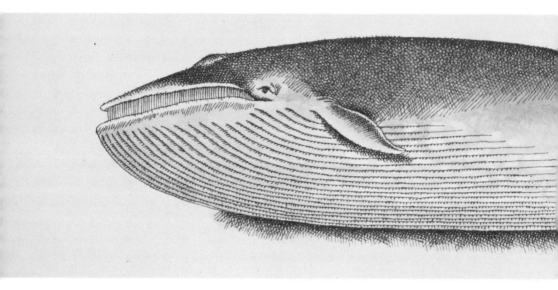

The baleen whales are a much smaller group than the toothed whales. There are many fewer kinds. But nearly all the baleen whales are great whales. One of them, the blue whale, is the largest animal on earth.

Fully grown, a blue whale is 85 to 100 or more feet long. It is bigger than a railroad steam engine. It is longer than the longest dinosaur.

Blue whale (above) is the largest animal on earth. It may grow to 100 feet long and weigh 300,000 pounds.

A blue whale spends the summer feeding. By summer's end, it may weigh 300,000 pounds or more. It weighs as much as 25 elephants. It is three times as heavy as the heaviest dinosaur.

This giant's tongue is bigger than a taxicab.

Its heart weighs half a ton.

The blue whale is not only the largest animal now alive. It is probably the largest animal that has ever lived. It is one of the wonders of the world.

Most of today's blue whales live in the Southern Hemisphere. In spring they swim to the cold waters off Antarctica. They spend the summer there, feeding on krill. When they arrive, they are very thin. But they eat steadily all summer, feasting on small shrimplike creatures. In a few months a blue whale may gain some 30 or 40 tons.

When autumn comes, all the blue whales leave the Antarctic. They swim north to warmer waters, and they spread out. Mates stay together, but blue whales do not live in groups.

The young are probably born in winter, when the whales are in warm waters. A newborn blue whale has no blubber. It might die of cold in Antarctic waters.

Even without blubber, a baby blue whale is huge. At birth it is about 25 feet long and it weighs 3 tons. It is nursed by its mother for about seven months. The mother whale produces a large supply of very rich milk. The baby grows at a rate of 200 pounds a day. By the time it stops nursing, it is 53 feet long and weighs about 24 tons.

The blue whale belongs to a family of whales called rorquals. *Rorqual* comes from a Norwegian word meaning "tubed whale." The name describes the whale's throat. The throat has deep pleats that look like tubes. The pleats open up when a whale is feeding. They let the whale take extra large mouthfuls of food.

A sleeping fin whale

There are six great whales in the rorqual family. Five of them are close relatives. They are the blue whale and the smaller, slimmer fin whale, which is the second biggest whale. Then there are three still smaller whales: the sei whale, the minke whale, and

Bryde's whale. So far as is known, all live in much the same way.

The sixth great whale in this family is the humpback whale. Like the other rorquals, it has a pleated throat. But in other ways it is different.

About 50 feet long, the humpback has a thick, chunky body. It has very long, narrow flippers. They are white, with scallops along the edges. The humpback also has lumps on its head, jaw, and flippers.

The humpback is the most playful of all the great whales. It leaps out of the water, then it falls flat with a huge crash and splash. It may turn a somersault above the water. Sometimes it swims on its back.

At mating time, pairs of humpbacks lie side by side in the water. They

On the following page, a humpback leaps into the air. This is the most playful of the great whales.

rub each other with their flippers. They give each other love pats that can be heard miles away.

The humpback is also the noisy baleen whale. Humpbacks make loud rumbling, grunting, wailing sounds. The sounds form a pattern. They make a song, much as a bird's notes do. Each humpback seems to have at least one song that it sings.

What do the songs mean? How do humpbacks use them? How far do the songs travel through the water? These are just a few of the things scientists are trying to find out.

Besides the rorquals, there are two other families of baleen whales.

One is made up only of the gray whales. They are found in the North Pacific. There seem to be two populations of gray whales. In summer both feed in Arctic waters. In autumn one travels to the waters around Korea. The other heads south to the bays of Baja California.

The other family is made up of right whales, which are also called

Greenland right whale may grow to be 60 feet long. Its huge head is one-third of its length.

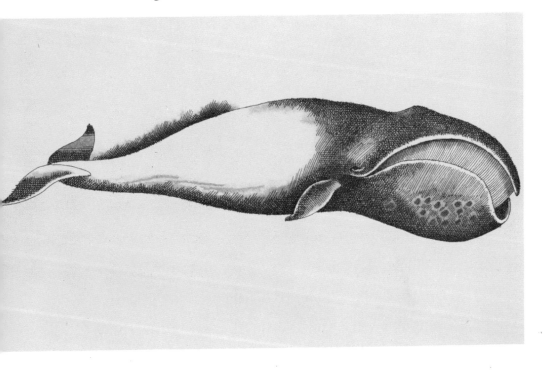

bowheads. Two of the right whales are great whales. They may grow to a length of 60 feet. Their baleen is 13 to 15 feet long—the longest of any baleen whale. A right whale has a big head with a mouth that looks as if it had been put on upside down.

The right whales got their name in the early days of whaling. They were the easiest whales to catch, and so they were the "right" ones to go after. Today they are the rarest of the great whales.

It is years since any whaling nation has hunted right whales. Why are there so few? Why haven't they been able to make a comeback?

That is one of the many, many things that scientists hope to learn about great whales—if there is time.

5. TIME TO LEARN?

Once there were many, many great whales in all the oceans of the world. Today their numbers are much smaller. In the last 50 years alone, more than two million great whales have been killed.

How many are left? No one knows. But scientists in many countries fear for the great whales. They fear that some kinds will die out and disappear forever.

The blue whale is one of these. Among whalers, the blue whale was too big for its own good. It was the biggest whale and so it was the biggest prize. Today there are few blue whales left. There may be so few that they cannot find mates.

Most of the big whaling nations stopped their hunting some years ago. They did not have to have whale oil or whale meat. There were other products that could be used instead.

But two countries did not stop. They were Japan and the Soviet Union. Their whaling ships kept up the hunt.

Mostly they hunted in the Antarctic in summer. The waters held both rorquals and sperm whales. If one kind of whale grew scarce, there were other kinds to hunt.

The rorquals were greatly harmed. Whole populations of them summered

Minke whale is the smallest of the rorquals. It grows to a length of just over 30 feet.

in the Antarctic. There were adult whales, young whales, and calves. Some of the adults were females carrying babies. When they were killed, the unborn babies were lost. Calves lost their mothers. Young whales were killed before they had ever mated or had calves. And so the number of rorquals grew smaller and smaller.

The sperm whales in the Antarctic were all males. They were young males that had no herds. They were old males that had lost their herds. Hunting them was not as harmful as hunting cows and calves. Even so, the number of sperm whales has grown smaller and smaller.

And still the killing goes on.

The story of man and the great whales is not a nice one. Some men seem willing to wipe out the earth's largest animals. If the great whales disappear, the earth will have lost another of its treasures. And we shall have lost animals from which we have much to learn.

So far, we know little about the great whales. It is hard to study animals that live in the sea. There is no way to follow them and watch them through the year. There is no way to live among them.

Minke is hauled aboard a Japanese whaling ship.

Most of what we know has been learned from dead whales. Scientists are only beginning to study living whales. The studies have taught us about the clicks of sperm whales and the songs of humpbacks. But there are many questions about whales for which we have no answers.

For example, we know most about the size and weight of blue whales. But where are blue whales born? How often does a female have a calf? Do blue whales mate for life? Where and how do they find mates? Where do they spend the winter? How deep can they dive? How do they find their way through the ocean? How do they find one another? When do they sleep? What diseases do they have? Why has cancer never been found in a blue whale? How long do blue whales live? How long can they grow? How intelligent are they? With luck, there may be time to learn the answers to these questions.

At present, we know most about certain small whales, such as dolphins. They are small enough to capture, feed, and study. Only once has a great whale been studied this way. Only once have people come to know a great whale. And the whale, who was named Gigi, chose two of them to be her friends.

Gigi, the star of Sea World, takes a look around.

6. THE FRIENDLY WHALE

Gigi was a young California gray whale. She was captured in Scammon Lagoon when she was only a baby. The men who caught her did not mean her any harm. They wanted to study her. And so they took her to Sea World, a park at San Diego. There she was put in a big round tank full of salt water.

The tank had to be big. Gigi might have been a baby, but she was eighteen feet long and weighed 4,300 pounds. A 4,300-pound baby needs a lot of food. Sea World fed Gigi a mixture of heavy cream, ground fish and squid, cod-liver oil, vitamins, yeast, and water.

At first Gigi lost weight. But then she began to grow. Every day she grew a third of an inch and gained 27 pounds.

Sea World gave Gigi a dolphin for company. It also sent her some of its Sea Maids, who were girl swimmers. They, too, swam with her. Gigi seemed happy. She swam and jumped and rolled as a young whale should.

A friendship began between Gigi and a man named Bud, who was taking care of her.

First Bud discovered that Gigi liked

Gigi about to be fed. Note baleen, eyes, blowholes.

him to rub her. He would rub her from head to tail.

Next Bud began to train Gigi. He used pats as signals. One pat meant that she was to pay attention. Two pats meant that she was to open her mouth. Three pats meant "no" or "be quiet." Gigi learned the signals. She would move where Bud wanted her when he was feeding her or cleaning the tank.

Before long, Gigi learned to feed herself. She would suck squid up from the floor of her tank. To do this, she turned on her side and opened one side of her mouth. She sucked in the squid and raised her tongue to squirt out the water. Then she swallowed the squid.

Gigi took food from people who were

Gigi learned to suck up squid from floor of tank.

swimming beside her. She would open her mouth for Bud to feed her.

Bud learned many interesting things about Gigi. One was that she didn't like mackerel—and she could tell one kind of food from another. Fed mackerel and squid, Gigi would swallow the squid and spit out the mackerel.

Bud also found that Gigi made at least four kinds of sounds. Her happy sound was a big deep grunt.

Sometimes scientists came to study Gigi. They tried to handle her. Gigi

Like all whales, Gigi could swim beneath or at surface.

Gigi always knew Bud, even when he was in a wet suit.

would make such a fuss that they had
to stop and send for Bud. As soon
as Bud came, Gigi calmed down.

Gigi also had a second friend. This
was one of the Sea Maids, a girl
named Sue. Sue was good at feeding
Gigi. She swam with Gigi. She petted
Gigi. And Gigi would take Sue for
rides, swimming round and round the

Sue could climb on Gigi's back and go for a ride.

Gigi would stop or go on signals from Sue.

tank. She would stop or go on signals from Sue. When Gigi tired of giving a ride, she simply rolled over and Sue fell off.

By the time Gigi had spent a year at Sea World, she had grown greatly. She was 27 feet long and weighed nearly seven tons. Her food was costing $200 a day.

That was too much. Sea World decided that Gigi would have to go back in the sea. She would have to go soon, before she grew too big to be moved.

A scientist made the plans. He decided Gigi should be moved in the spring. At that time other gray whales would be passing by the California coast, traveling north. He hoped Gigi could join them.

The scientist worked out a way to attach a small package to Gigi's back. It was to send out radio signals so that Gigi could be tracked.

Early one March morning, a sling was wrapped around the whale. A crane lifted her out of the tank. She was put down in a big truck and covered with wet blankets. Bud and Sue rode with Gigi. They patted her and talked to her and kept her calm.

A barge carried Gigi out to sea. A crane lowered her into the water. Bud dived in and pulled the sling away. He swam beside her until she dived.

Gigi surfaced and made a wide circle around the boat. Then she started north. There were other whales nearby.

The radio signals were tracked for

Helped by Bud, Gigi sets out for a home in the sea.

more than two weeks. By then Gigi
had traveled over 500 miles. She was
swimming north with the other gray
whales.

Gigi, the friendly whale, was gone.
She had joined her own kind and
taken up the life of a great whale.

INDEX